# Planning and Surviving Retirement

*Written by*
Adrienne Gottlieb, J.D.

Planning and Surviving Retirement
Copyright © 2020 by Adrienne Gottlieb
ISBN 13: 978-1-949993-22-6

A Publication of the Gottlieb Insurance Group

Available from Amazon.com and other retail outlets. Orders by U.S. trade bookstores and wholesalers. Quantity sales special discounts are available on quantity purchases by corporations, associations, and others. For details, contact the publisher at the address above.

Cover art & overall book design by Aaron Jones.

Printed in the USA.
01 20                    10 9 8 7 6 5 4 3 2 1

# Contents

# Contents

# Introduction

This book is written so that what happened to me won't happen to you. As you will read later in the book, my retirement planning and retirement funds took big hits in 1999 and in 2008. I didn't know that the programs and products explained in this book even existed. If only I had known!

If you subject your retirement funds to market loss and you don't know when the market will take a turn for the worse (who does?), how do you know those funds will be there when you retire?

You see, retirement is about income (and health). By the time you reach your late 60's or early 70's; should the market take a hit, you don't have the years left to ride it out. Your peak earning years are probably over.

# Introduction

Besides waiting out the market is a very old investment plan. Times have changed and volatility seems to be the rule now. You can avoid that pitfall.

You can protect your retirement funds and you can safely plan for and survive retirement. Read on.

# ARE YOU TIRED OF LOSING YOUR RETIREMENT MONEY IN THE MARKET OR...

# ...PLAYING CATCH-UP WHEN YOU DO?

*"The starting point of all achievement is desire."*
— *Napoleon Hill*

CARDS

GET WELL

"Do you have a 'Get Better Soon' card
for someone's retirement investment?"

*Chapter 1*

# WHY RISK YOUR RETIREMENT MONEY?

**W**hy risk your retirement money in the market? The consequences of another 2008 crash are dire if you plan on retiring. Here are a few retirement challenges to consider.

- **Investor Blunders:** Americans tend to buy high and sell low! Vanguard, the people who invented the index fund, and other experts are expecting 3% to 5% moving forward which is 1% to 3% real after inflation. Is 1% worth the risk? Not really. We are basically now subsidizing the Fortune 500.

- **Healthcare Nightmare:** Because of the ever-increasing costs of medical care, Americans consider healthcare the single most critical national issue.

- **The Invisible Enemy:** The average annual rate of inflation since 1926 has been 3% but could be far greater in the coming decades.

- **Taxes:** This is the single largest household expense and the only place for taxes to go—is up!

- **Disappearing Pensions:** With the demise of company sponsored retirement plans, it has become incumbent upon us to save for our own retirement.

- **Social Security:** Will it be around when you retire? Is it paying out more than it takes in?

- **The Age Factor:** Americans are living longer and without proper preparation, we stand a high probability of outliving our financial resources.

Considering these challenges is not meant to depress you. There is light at the end of the tunnel and there are strategies to defeat the above challenges.

*"The best time to start thinking about your retirement is before the boss does."* — *Unknown*

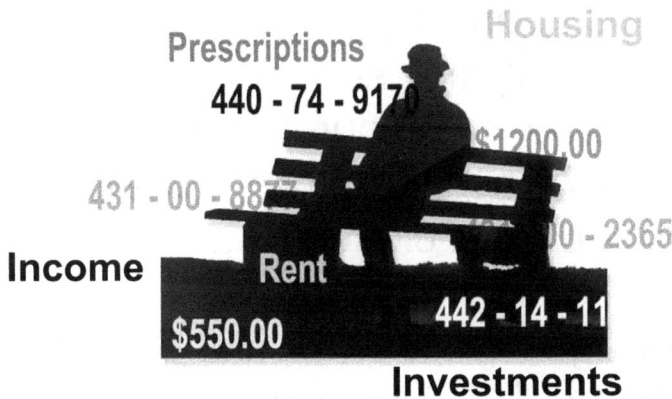

Prescriptions
440 - 74 - 91...
Housing
$1200.00
431 - 00 - 88...
...0 - 2365
Income
Rent
$550.00
442 - 14 - 11
Investments

*Chapter 2*

# SOCIAL SECURITY

L et's explore a couple of these challenges a bit more. First of all: **Social Security** is NOT the financial lifeline you think it is.

Millions of seniors today collect Social Security in retirement and use those benefits to help pay their living costs.

But if you're nearing your senior years without much or any savings, you should know that those benefits can't bail you out as you might expect. The sooner you recognize that, the sooner you can take steps to improve your financial picture – and avoid a cash-strapped existence once your career closes out.

The average senior on Social Security today collects $17,748 a year in benefits. Compare that number to your current annual income and see how the numbers line up. You'll see that it equates to barely more than the minimum wage in most states, and living on that sum would probably mean making a host of lifestyle sacrifices you're not keen on doing.

Here's another way of looking at it: Social Security will replace about 40% of your pre-retirement income if you're an average wage earner. But most seniors need roughly double that amount to live comfortably.

When you think about what your senior expenses will look like, you'll see why.

Though it's true that many retirees manage to pay off their homes before leaving the workforce, even if you're able to do the same, the rest of your current expenses will likely continue to apply after your career ends.

Sure, you might save some money on fuel costs to account for not having to commute, but chances are that you'll still need a car and the insurance that comes with it. You'll also need to pay for home maintenance and repairs, property taxes, food, utilities, and clothing. And if you're used to a heavily subsidized health insurance plan through your employer, you'll probably find that your healthcare expenses go up in retirement under Medicare.

The takeaway? Planning to live on 40% of your income may not be feasible, desirable, or realistic. And that's why you can't neglect to save for retirement and look to Social Security to make up for it.

If you're nearing retirement with little money in your 401(k) or IRA, don't give up. As long as you still have an income, you have a chance to build some savings. And having some money in your nest egg is better than having none.

Social Security may be a valuable source of income for seniors, but you can't live on it alone. Acknowledging that sooner rather than later will put you in a better position to salvage your senior years and avoid financial troubles throughout them.

*Chapter 3*

# RETIREMENT PLANS

Americans aren't coming close to maxing out their **Retirement Plans** New data from GOBankingRates reveals that Americans aren't saving enough for their golden years. Currently, IRAs max out at $6,000 a year for workers under 50, and $7,000 a year for those 50 and older. Meanwhile, 401(k) contribution limits max out at $19,000 a year for workers under 50, and $25,000 a year for the 50-and-over set -- and, they're going up in 2020. Yet the typical worker's annual retirement contribution today doesn't even hit the halfway point on the IRA limit. And that means today's savers need to do better.

Today's workers aren't coming close to maxing out their retirement plans, there's a variance in contribution levels by age:

Age Range Average Annual Retirement Plan Contribution:

18-24 — $2,107.59
25-34 — $1,758.88
35-44 — $2,250.12
45-54 — $2,739.19
55-64 — $2,333.76
65 and older — $784.32

Oddly enough, workers between the ages of 18 and 24 seem to manage higher contributions than those between the ages of 25 to 34. That could be due in part to the fact that millennials in this age range are starting families, and as such, have less money left over to fund their retirement savings after child care costs and other kid-related expenses are accounted for. It's also not surprising to see that those 65 and over aren't contributing a whole lot to their savings. Many people in that age range are working part-time at best, or are gearing up to withdraw from their nest eggs rather than build them. But all told, workers need to be more aggressive in their savings efforts if they want to retire comfortably.

If someone around 40 managed to save an average of $288/month for 45 years, they could have over $700,000 in retirement, assuming an average of 7% return. The problem is most people will not save for 45 years. If we assume he or she managed to save for 25 years, the balance at retirement would just be slightly over $170,000. Quite a difference.

The point? The closer workers of all ages get to maxing out their annual retirement plan contributions, the more financial security they'll buy themselves.

While setting aside some amount of money for retirement is better than socking away none at all, today's workers should make an effort to eke out additional savings. Otherwise, they really risk struggling once their golden years roll around.

*Chapter 4*
# VOLATILE MARKETS

So how is one to protect oneself through **Volatile Markets** and preserve enough money for a comfortable retirement?

In 2019, we have witnessed frequent volatility in the U.S. markets — dramatic fluctuation in share prices that can undermine portfolio values.

Such market gyrations are unnerving to many investors, but perhaps none more so than those who are retired or about to retire. Retirement is typically the beginning of the decumulation stage, when paychecks from work stop and retirees begin withdrawing money from their retirement accounts. Because their investment horizon is more immediate, these investors are particularly vulnerable to sharp declines in the markets. Sequence-of-returns risk – where the timing of withdrawals may have a negative impact on the overall value of the retirement account – can have significant long-term consequences on a retiree's life. Not only can a market downturn erode retirement cash flows, but many retirees and would be retirees also don't have as much time as younger investors for their portfolios to rebound.

Take a look at this simple equation. 100 – 30 + 43 = 0. Let me explain. Assume you invested $100 in a stock which then declined by 30%. (Think 2008) It would then take a 43% increase to bring the stock value back up to even. Hence the zero – you would have made nothing. And how long would it take for 43% growth? Who knows? A year? 2 years? 10 years?

Given the historical frequency of market volatility in the U.S. stock market, investors should weigh the prospect of it occurring when they are about to retire or have already retired. One important way for clients to help shield themselves against sequence risk is to ensure that a portion of their planned retirement income is protected from the ups and downs of the market and guaranteed to last as long as they live. It's not surprising then that Americans are increasingly looking for guaranteed income options to protect themselves.

If you are some of the lucky ones, pensions are one of those sources of protected lifetime income. However, today only 17% of Americans have access to one. Social Security is another source of lifetime income, but many people don't realize that it only replaces an average of 40% of our pre-retirement paycheck, leaving a large income gap that needs to be filled.

*"The question isn't at what age I want to retire, it's at what income." - George Foreman*

*Chapter 5*

# ANNUITIES

A nother source of protected lifetime income, one that can help protect income against volatile markets and sequence risk, is the guaranteed income benefit that a fixed **annuity** can provide. Annuities are a proven and smart way for people to protect their income, knowing they'll always have a "monthly check" to count on every month, regardless of the ups and downs of the markets. Annuities also have the potential for market growth without market risk.

# Solutions

Safety    Growth

Income

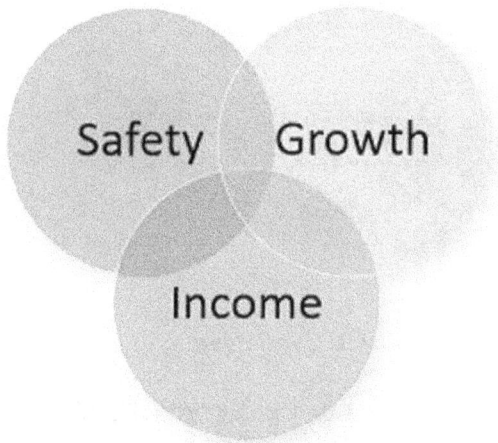

I have found that part of the reason people often miss the very best in life is that they hold misconceptions and falsehoods closely as truth. It may be because of a parent or a teacher, a book or a TV Show, but somewhere along the line people create a series of truths that become inviolable; but in fact, are completely false.

Here's an example. "If you pull out a gray hair ten more will grow back." It's funny, I know; but many still believe this. We hold on to something as true because someone simple stated it as fact. We trusted the person, so we never researched the issue ourselves. We never did our own homework. It simply became our reality, and we propagated it as truth to others as well, without so much as even a shred of proof.

When I tell you the **solution** to all of the challenges we have been discussing, you may have a negative reaction. You might hear the voice in your head of some previous financial advisor or talk show host whispering in your ear.

When I ask people why they believe what they do especially regarding finances and financial planning, they are really not sure why. Their usual answer is usually along the line of "that's what I have heard" or "that's what I have been told."

So what's my solution you ask. *It is my belief that the single best place to save and preserve retirement dollars is in a permanent life insurance contract or fixed (often times indexed) annuity product.*

Did you hear those voices in your head? Let's explore what I mean. Life insurance isn't just about dying.

*Chapter 6*

# Life Insurance

There are just two kinds of **life insurance** regardless of how many labels or names companies put on their products. You have probably heard of 10-year term, 20-year term, 30-year term, return-of-premium term, whole life, decreasing term, universal life, blah, blah, blah. There are still only 2 types: term and permanent.

## Term Insurance

Consider the following analogy. Think of term insurance like renting a home and permanent insurance life buying a home. The first characteristic of **term** insurance is that it is low cost (initially) just like renting a home.

The second characteristic of term insurance is that eventually the premium goes up over time. While each term policy is slightly different, at some point the premium will go up, just like rent on a home. When the lease is up, the rent goes up as well.

Another characteristic of term insurance is that it has no equity. When you decide to leave the rental, you get no money back except a small deposit (if you are lucky).

The fourth characteristic of term insurance is very significant. At some point in the future, even if you are still alive, the coverage will end. It might be when you are 80, 85, 90 or when a specified term like 20 years is over.

When do people need life insurance? Usually when they die! Unfortunately, most people die when they are much older. Therefore, these term policies terminate right when they are most needed. So all the money that has been paid in (just like rent) is thrown to the wind.

# PERMANENT INSURANCE

Most people shy away from **permanent** insurance because it has initially a higher cost than term insurance. However, the premium stays level; it never goes up!

A key feature of permanent insurance is that it builds equity or cash value. As well as cash value, permanent insurance never ends as long as you pay the premium.

When comparing these two types of insurance, than just like buying a home is financially wiser than renting, permanent insurance (if affordable) is by far wiser as well.

Life insurance and life insurance products can do far more than provide a death benefit. In fact, if structured properly, it can serve as one of the most powerful retirement strategies available anywhere.

*"Don't save what is left after spending but spend what is left after savings."* - *Warren Buffet*

*Chapter 7*

# RETIREMENT MONEY

W hen you retire, there will be either taxable or tax-free monies available to you. Taxable monies include stocks, mutual funds, or real estate which generate capital gains tax; and tax qualified plans (like a 401K) that generate income tax.

On the tax-free side of things are municipal bonds, Roth IRAs and Life Insurance. Frankly municipal bonds won't generate enough income for you these days so we are left with Roth IRAs and Life Insurance.

So, here is our question to answer "what can give me free money, tax-free money, and tax-deferred money or even taxable income when I retire?

Ah you say, my employer contributes to my 401K so that's free money. It even grows tax-deferred. But eventually, it will be taxable.

Let's look at that 401K that so many are relying on for retirement.

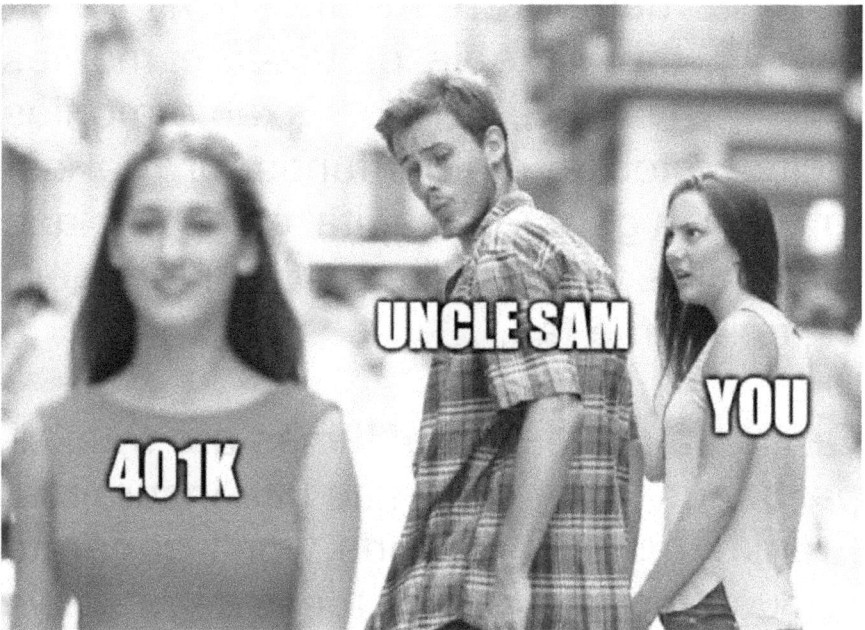

The average 401K exposes your money to 50% losses. READ THAT AGAIN. Half your retirement money gone. What would losing HALF your retirement savings money mean to your future. What would you do? You say that's ridiculous, I'm not going to lose half. Remember 2008? It wasn't that long ago and the market bubble today is even bigger than it was then. Furthermore, the market is more volatile than ever. Can you time your retirement with the market to make sure you only retire when your stocks are up? If so, I desperately need your secret!

And, what is the risk-return ration with your 401K? The average is 5.5% return. That's the average. You are shooting for less than 6% but you are risking 50% of your capital to get that tiny return. Down cycles in the market are wealth killers. You need to redistribute your 401K dollars into a bucket that will give you growth without the risk of loss, continue build tax-free and be liquid (without loss), as well as protect you from volatility. Well, that would certainly be less stressful, wouldn't it. Stick with me, we have a plan!

I'm not here to scare you. The self-destructive market is enough to do that. I am here to protect you and your investments, to protect your future and get you on the right track ASAP.

If you are following a market strategy for retirement, bear in mind that type of retirement and financial planning was developed in the 80's. A lot has changed in 40 years! I still remember when the bubble burst in 1999 as well at 2008. In 1999 the market hit all time highs and then declined 51%. And now we have grown into the longest bull market in history. You do have to ask yourself just one question. Do you feel lucky?! The easy money has been made. Bulls make money. Bears make money. Pigs get slaughtered!

*Chapter 8*

# WHAT CAN WE DO?

I told you previously that life insurance products can grow your money without risk and provide you with a very nice income in retirement. Let's briefly look at two of those product; the Indexed Universal Life Insurance Policy (IUL) and a Fixed Indexed Annuity (FIA).

## INDEXED UNIVERSAL LIFE INSURANCE

What if you could get the flexibility of adjustable life insurance premiums and face value and an opportunity to increase cash value—would you go for it? What if you could get this without the inherent downside risk of investing in the equities market? All of this is possible with an indexed universal life insurance policy. They allow the owner of the policy to allocate cash value amounts to either a fixed account or an equity index account. Policies offer a variety of well-known indexes such as the S&P 500 but no money is actually invested in equity positions. YOU WILL NEVER LOSE MONEY DUE TO A MARKET DECLINE (or "correction" like financial advisors like to call it) EVER. HOW GOOD IS THAT?

This is how they work. When a premium is paid, a portion pays for life insurance for the insured. Any fees are paid, and the rest is added to the cash value. The total amount of cash value is credited with interest based on increases in an equity index (but it is not directly invested in the stock market). Some policies allow the policyholder to select multiple indexes. IULs usually offer a guaranteed minimum fixed interest rate and a choice of indexes. Policyholders can decide the percentage allocated to the fixed and indexed accounts.

The bottom line: growth without market risk. It is that simple. Not just growth but compounded growth. When given adequate time, these policies generate substantial retirement money, not to mention a very important and lucrative legacy.

If a young professional begins one of these policies when in their twenties or thirties, there will be substantial money for retirement. If a parent or grandparent begins a child's life with an IUL, Katie bar the door! If you want to change the course of a family member's future, this is the way to do it!

# FIXED INDEXED ANNUITIES

Today Fixed Indexed Annuities (FIA) can not only grow your money for a period of time but also they can provide you with a guaranteed fixed income for life. They can also provide with an income for a period of time like 10, 20 or 25 years. The choice is yours.

Currently people are living longer, healthier lives and it's very likely they may spend a third of their lives in retirement. This makes it important for people close to retirement to ask the question: How can I guarantee lifetime income, no matter how long my life might be? Rolling your old 401K or any other monies you are saving and wanting to grow over into a FIA not only keeps your retirement money safe, but also it can grow without risk and provide you with the income necessary for an enjoyable retirement.

In the past, bonds served as the sole

answer to protection from loss. Advisors have long had a love/hate relationship with annuities. But with bond yields at such low levels, advisors are often at pains to find other ways of de-risking their clients' portfolios, especially as they approach retirement.

Keeping your retirement money safe from market loss, yet participating in market growth is key. Fixed Indexed Annuities can do just that.

An FIA can offer you both a potential source of guaranteed income in retirement and a growth vehicle that will outperform bonds—without the risk of loss of the initial investment. Talk about peace of mind!

With a FIA you'll earn stock market-linked interest returns if the market goes up. But if the market goes down, you are guaranteed to never lose a dime because if the following: 1. Your principle is backed by the assets of the insurance company issuing your annuity. 2. You are contractually guaranteed to earn a minimum amount of interest each year—no matter what! 3. all upside growth, which is credited to your account is locked in, normally on an annual basis, with no possibility of ever losing any of those gains, even if the market declines in the future.

As a cautionary consideration, annuities (FIA) are long-term vehicles designed for retirement purposes. They are not intended to replace emergency funds!

While a women-led revolution plays out in the American workplace, the retirement landscape is still evolving. Let's take a brief look at the challenges for women who retire.

*Chapter 9*

# OTHER ISSUES TO CONSIDER

There are several issues to consider when planning for retirement. Gender is one. So is considering how long you might live; what are your family genes like, are you male or female, state of your health, and the increasing cost of healthcare. All of these factors should at least be discussed and considered where appropriate. Another issue is your tolerance for risk. Are you comfortable risking retirement money? In other words, are you already independently wealthy? Probably not or you wouldn't be reading this book! Let's briefly look at some of these issues.

# WOMEN IN RETIREMENT

In the second half of the 20th century, women's participation in the workforce rose from just under 30% to almost 47%. Today, women continue to make up nearly half of the workforce in the U.S., own more than 1 million businesses, and are the sole or primary breadwinners for 42% of families with children under 18.

Despite this, women face a reality different from their counterparts in life after work. Let's take a look at some of the factors defining this disparity and see what can help.

# GENDER GAP IN RETIREMENT

Women often face bigger challenges in retirement because of leaving the workforce to raise children or care for elderly rela-

tives. This often leads to fewer years contributing to an employer-sponsored retirement account.

Further exacerbating this situation is a gender pay gap rooted in the years when the
vast majority of women have children (late
20s to mid-30s). According to one study,
the gender pay gap for college graduates,
which starts close to zero, widens by more
than 50% before narrowing again as we
near retirement.

The National Institute on Retirement Security reports that women age 65 and
older typically make 25% less than men.
Women are 80% more likely than men to
be impoverished at age 65, while women
75 to 79 are 3 times more likely than men
to be living in poverty.

# LONGEVITY

According to HealthView Services, a health
care cost projection firm, a healthy 30 year

old woman is projected to spend almost $120,000.00 more than a healthy 30 year old man to cover healthcare costs during their lives. This is due in part to longevity where higher health care costs are incurred in the final four years of life.

A man reaching age 65 today can expect to live, on average, until age 84.3. A woman turning age 65 today can expect to live on average until 86.6. Moreover, about one out of every four 65-year-olds today will live past age 90, and one out of every 10, past age 95.

# PRIORITIES

According to some studies, women are less likely than men to rank saving for retirement at the top of their financial priorities. Instead, women place general costs, paying off debts and housing costs as a higher priority. The disparity may stem from division of labor at home. Nevertheless, this schism can wreak havoc on long-term planning as married and un-married women age into retirement.

If you are a woman who hopes to retire one day, is nearing retirement, or is in re-tirement then you need to speak with me about a plan that grows and preserves your retirement funds. In all honesty, the longer you wait to address retirement is-sues, the greater your risk of not having a secure retirement.

*"Someone is sitting in the shade today because some-one planted a tree a long time ago."*

*— Warren Buffet*

*Chapter 10*

# CLOSING THE GAP

T he safe money options we have been discussing are available for alternative income solutions that offer tax deferral, no contribution limits and nest egg growth.

Quite frankly, if you are aged 25-45, you need an IUL; period. The cost of this insurance is low and it enables you to buy retirement dollars at half-price or less.

If you are between the ages of 45 to 65 and older, you need to protect the retirement money you have. The only sure way to do that is with a FIA that guarantees you the return of your investment and most often a return on your investment.

I am a retired lawyer. Retired in 2007. Guess what happened to my retirement money. You got it. Lost about 35% of it in the 2008 crash. Even though it's been 12 years, have I caught up? No, not really. The brokers will tell you otherwise but not all of your stocks or funds or whatever they were pushing at the time will catch up. In 2007, we thought the only way was up.

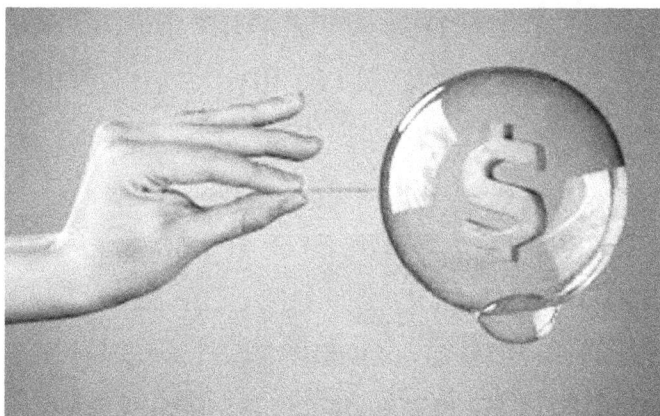

And we are in the same situation in 2020. Only this time, the bubble is bigger. The question of when the bubble will burst is not "if," but "when." You can prepare for it and you can protect yourself from it, if you are willing.

*"Retirement is wonderful if you have two essentials — much to live on and much to live for." – Unknown*

# ABOUT ME

I don't know you, but you can know me. Visit my web site at:

*www.gottliebinsurancegroup.com*

Read my bio and then you need to call me. It doesn't matter what state you are in, I am licensed in that state.

Take the steps now to secure your future. If you have an old 401K sitting in your old employer's account, making him or her look good to their broker, roll it over into a self-directed IRA that is a Fixed Indexed Annuity. There is no fee or charge for you to do that regardless of what your "financial advisor" tells you. And yes, someone like me makes a commission for selling you one of these annuities or universal life policies. However it is a one time commission paid by the insurance company and does NOT come out of your funds nor is there a yearly fee to "manage" your account!

Investigate what I have told you and contact me to discuss a tailored-to-your-specific-needs plan so that you can prepare for and enjoy your retirement. Retirement is about income and health. Don't neglect either.

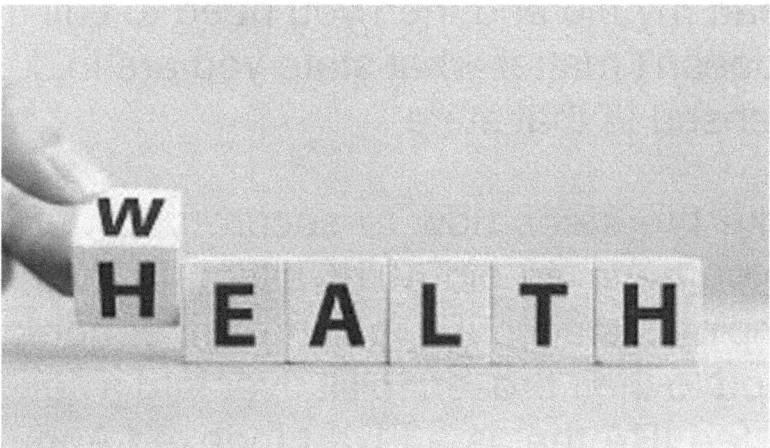

www.ingramcontent.com/pod-product-compliance
Lightning Source LLC
Chambersburg PA
CBHW050548210326
41520CB00012B/2760